GW00492613

Mum

Yes
YOU
CAN!

Compiled by Marc Anello

Illustrated by Jenny Faw

 PETER PAUPER PRESS, INC.
WHITE PLAINS, NEW YORK

Book designed by Arlene Greco
Illustrations copyright © 1998 Jenny Faw

Text copyright © 1998
Peter Pauper Press, Inc.
202 Mamaroneck Avenue
White Plains, NY 10601
ISBN 0-88088-841-5
Printed in China
7 6 5 4 3 2 1

YES
YOU CAN!

The purpose of life
is a life of purpose.

Robert Byrne

Life is to be lived,
not analyzed.
Time is to be used,
not wasted.

Lauren Bacall

Learn to take risks.
They can be the most exciting
events of your life, as you
soar toward your goals.

Nancy Foreman

Confidence . . .
translates into power.

Trisha Yearwood

I'm a glutton
for life.

Gladys Knight

I'm happiest when
I'm working,
rising to challenges.

Lucille Ball

The only way I know to get
a good show is to practice,
sweat, rehearse and worry. . . .
You have to plug away, keep
thinking up new ideas. If one
doesn't work, try another.

Fred Astaire

Excellence is not an act
but a habit. The things you
do the most are the
things you will do best.

Marva Collins

There is no failure in life other than not trying. If you want something badly enough, make an attempt. . . . A lot of people get scared. They're afraid to fail. Take that word out of your vocabulary. You didn't "fail." You "tried your best."

Jane Seymour

Never mistake motion
for action.

Ernest Hemingway

Whenever I'd get ready to call it a day, I'd think, "No. Somebody else is still practicing. Somebody—*somewhere*—is playing that extra ten or fifteen minutes . . . I don't know if I practiced more than *anybody*, but I sure practiced enough.

Larry Bird

A star is not something that
flashes through the sky.
That's a comet. Or a meteor.
A star is something you can
steer ships by. It stays in place
and gives off a steady glow; it
is fixed, permanent. A star
works at being a star.

Jim Murray

In the beginning was the Note,
and the Note was with God.
Whosoever can reach for that
Note, reach high, and bring it
back to us on earth . . .

Leonard Bernstein

Some people think I work too
hard but the important thing
for me is to keep going. . . .
Whether you are twenty-four,
sixty-four, or seventy-four,
makes no difference. The only
thing that counts is how
good the show is.

Irving Berlin

Maybe the day will come
when I can sit back and be
content . . . But until that day
comes, I intend to stay in the
batter's box—I don't let the
big guys push me out of
there anymore—and keep
hammering away.

Hank Aaron

I think the challenge is to take
. . . difficult and painful times
and turn them into something
beneficial, something that
makes you grow.

Michelle Akers

You have to be very clear what
you want in order to succeed.

Hazelle Goodman

The condition of the human spirit [is] so profound that it encourages us to build bridges.

Maya Angelou

Success is not so much
achievement as achieving.
Refuse to join the cautious
crowd that plays not to
lose; play to win.

David J. Mahoney

The reason why birds can fly
and we can't is simply that they
have perfect faith, for to have
faith is to have wings.

James M. Barrie

You've got to persevere.
Persevere, and keep
your sense of humor.

Jim Brady

I think I've basically played
for an idea, which is how close
I could come to being at my
best. I put some hard
work into that.

Kareem Abdul-Jabbar

Living life intensely
has a momentum and
exhilaration of its own. . . .
I've always preferred moving
to sitting still.

Bill Bradley

I must not only try harder, but
be better. . . . You are playing
yourself, your own highest
standards, and when you reach
your limits, that is the real joy.

Arthur Ashe

I don't stop at anything. I start
with the idea that nothing is
impossible and everything can
be done in the end.

Alberta Ferretti

My mission is to leave behind
me the kind of impression
that will make it easier for
those who follow.

Marian Anderson

What I aspire to is to touch
people on a very simple level,
to move them and to
move their hearts.

Julie Taymor

I don't mind
proving myself.

Melba Moore

I see how important it is
to live a life where you
are really committed.

Anita Hill

We must be more grateful for
all the little things in life—
walking, talking, moving,
loving. Don't give up,
and you have a chance.

Kirk Douglas

When and how I have lived is
unimportant. It is what I have
done with where I have been
that should be of interest.

Georgia O'Keeffe

I wasn't about being rich
or famous. I just wanted to be
somebody. I was absolutely
driven. I was going to succeed.

Jenny Jones

It's lack of faith that makes
people afraid of meeting
challenges . . .

Muhammad Ali

People who use their energies
negatively or positively, those
energies are there to be used
and they will apply, somehow.

Marlon Brando

To be good was more
important than to be rich.
To be kind was more important
than owning a house or a car.
To respect one's work and to do
it well, to risk something in
life, was more important
than being a star.

Lauren Bacall

I've had a lot of happiness,
and I'm not afraid to
expect more . . .

Carol Burnett

The biggest things are always
the easiest to do because there
is no competition.

William Van Horne

I made most things happen
for me, and if they were good,
I worked to get them. . . .
I lived the way I wanted to
live . . . Let the world know
you as you are . . .

Fanny Brice

The more you challenge
yourself, the more you learn to
do, the more your self-esteem
really shoots up: Hey! I can
do this! You're a success.

Mary Ann Goff

Enjoy what you have now to
the fullest. In all honesty you
really only have two choices;
you can like what you do *OR*
you can dislike it. I choose to
like it and what fun I have had.

Barbara Bush

With a bit of courage and
a dash of self-discipline,
a small talent can go
a long, long way.

Kitty Carlisle Hart

I'm always the heroine
of whatever I think about—
and everything always
turns out really good.

Cher

I've learned . . . to never take my eyes off the goal. I hate the word "can't." "Can't" is like a disease that keeps you from doing things. . . . I'm happy for myself. I've had my dreams come true, and that's what's important.

Chris Burke

The bird that flies out of the
ashes ... will rise from the
ashes on new wings.

Judy Collins

Cherish life for all its simplicity
as well as its grandeur. . . .
"GO and DO" is our motto,
because ya never know!

Fran Drescher

Once in a while we stand tall
enough to touch the sky, look
the sun straight in the eye and
laugh. To me, this laughter is
the finest sound there is. It is
the sound of the human spirit,
the sound of life. It's the best
thing about us . . .

Linda Ellerbee

I've gained enough experience
to work anywhere and to relate
to people on all levels. . . .
And I've gained a great deal
of confidence in myself.

Aretha Franklin

I don't think there's anything as
wonderful in life as being able
to help someone else.

Betty Ford

It is people, not things, that are
life's most valued treasures.

Betz Hutchison

The learning process is
never-ending, and growth
will continue if only you
will allow it to.

Arlene Francis

It is by that which
cannot be taken away that
we can measure ourselves.

Mia Farrow

The future is whatever
we want it to be.

Geraldine A. Ferraro

I'm going to try to find out the
new ideas before the others do.

Ella Fitzgerald

I like to think that each of us
has his own little destiny and
we have to seek it—no one will
hand it to us.

Richard Chamberlain

I would rather sing one day as a lion than 100 years as a sheep.

Cecilia Bartoli

Exploration is the key. . . . the
journey is worth making for
what each of us might learn
about this remarkable union of
mind, body, and spirit that is
the human being.

Bill Moyers

We must use time as a tool,
not as a couch.

John F. Kennedy

One's life has value so long
as one attributes value to the
life of others, by means of love,
friendship, indignation
and compassion.

Simone de Beauvoir

They are able who
think they are able.

Virgil

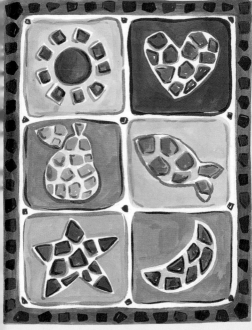

I am just myself, and
who I am is a lot.

Phylicia Rashad

Having once decided to achieve
a certain task, achieve it at all
costs of tedium and distaste.
The gain in self-confidence of
having accomplished a tiresome
labor is immense.

Arnold Bennett

He who laughs, lasts.

Robert Fulghum

If one's reputation is
a possession, then of all my
possessions, my reputation
means most to me.

Arthur Ashe

No one has more potential for
greatness than anyone else.

Marianne Williamson

I began to understand that
self-esteem isn't everything;
it's just that there's nothing
without it.

Gloria Steinem

The hardest thing is
to get started but the
really hardest thing
is to finish.

Yogi Berra